Twinkle, Twinkle, Little Star

by Jane Taylor

Illustrated by Julia Noonan

SCHOLASTIC INC.

New York   Toronto   London   Auckland   Sydney

Library of Congress Cataloging-in-Publication Data

Taylor, Jane, 1783–1824.
Twinkle, twinkle, little star / by Jane Taylor ; illustrated by
Julia Noonan.
p.   cm.
Summary: In this version of the familiar nineteenth-century poem,
the illustrations depict Santa Claus and his elves following a star
to the home of two children who eagerly await their visit.
ISBN 0-590-45566-4
1. Stars—Juvenile poetry.   2. Children's poetry, English.
[1. Stars—Poetry.   2. Santa Claus—Poetry.   3. Christmas—Poetry.
4. English poetry.]   I. Noonan, Julia, ill.   II. Title.
PR5549.T2T87   1992
821′.7—dc20   91-46898   CIP   AC

12   11   10   9   8   7   6   5   4   3   2   1   2   3   4   5   6   7/9
Printed in Singapore.

First Scholastic printing, October 1992

To John, who has always made my
Christmas wishes come true

Special thanks to Jim Roginski

*T*winkle, twinkle, little star,

How I wonder what you are!

★

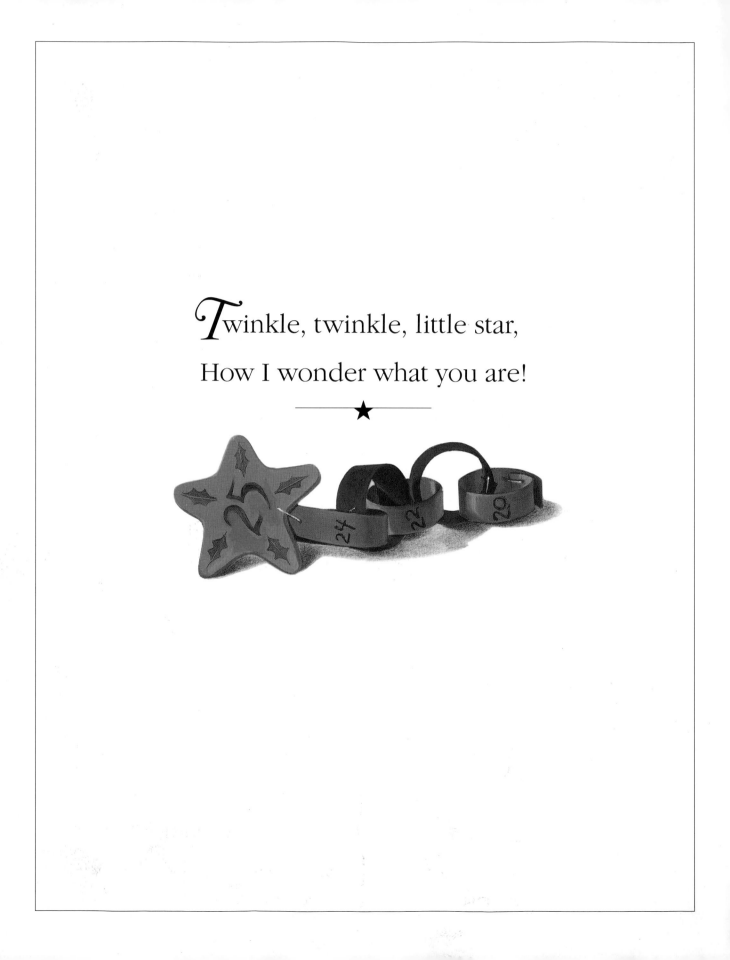

Up above the world so high,

Like a diamond in the sky.

★

When the blazing sun is gone,

When he nothing shines upon,

★

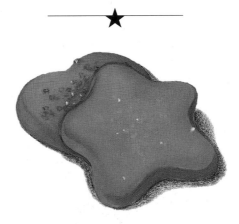

Then you show your little light,

Twinkle, twinkle, all the night.

★

Then the traveller in the dark,

Thanks you for your tiny spark;

★

He could not see which way to go,

If you did not twinkle so.

———★———

In the dark blue sky you keep,

And often through my curtains peep,

★

For you never shut your eye,

Till the sun is in the sky.

——————★——————

As your bright and tiny spark,

Lights the traveller in the dark,

———★———

Though I know not what you are,

Twinkle, twinkle, little star.

★

Twinkle, Twinkle, Little Star

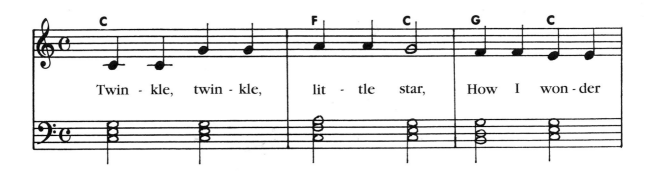

Twin - kle, twin - kle, lit - tle star, How I won - der

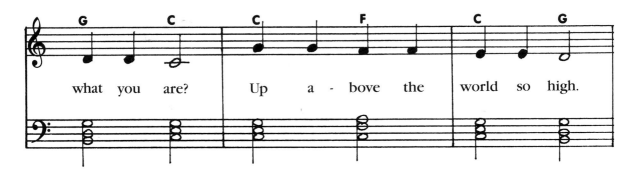

what you are? Up a - bove the world so high.

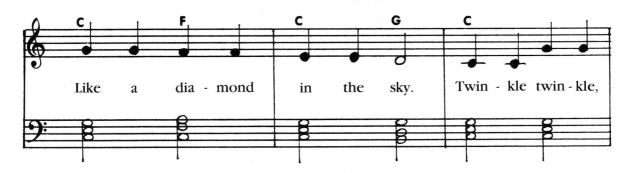

Like a dia - mond in the sky. Twin - kle twin - kle,

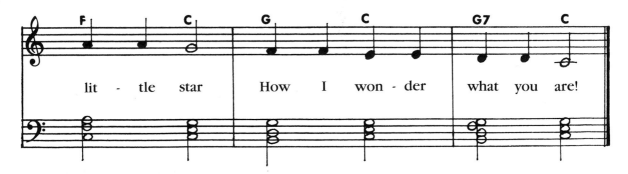

lit - tle star How I won - der what you are!

Merry Christmas love Julia